AF265882

The Scoop About Birthday Soup

*Using a child's creative side
to start a family tradition*

HOLLIS L. GREEN

GreenWine Family Books™
A division of
GlobalEdAdvancePress
37321-7635 USA

Library of Congress Control Number: 2008903881

Green, Hollis L., 1933--
The Scoop About Birthday Soup
ISBN 978-0-9796019-8-9
Subject Codes and Description: 1: JNF026100 - Juvenile Nonfiction: Holidays - Celebrations - Birthdays 2: PRD014000 - Periodicals: Craft/Hobby - General   3: CKB079000 - Cooking: Courses & Dishes

Printed in the United States of America

Published by
GreenWine Family Books
a division of
GlobalEdAdvancePress
37321-7635 USA

Dedicated to

Erin Elizabeth Sise

and

Children everywhere
who want to make
birthday soup

Children's Books
A subdivision of
GreenWine Family Books[T]
Books that adults enjoy reading to children and
children enjoy reading again and again.

HELLO!
MY NAME IS ERIN,
AND ONCE UPON A BIRTHDAY

MY AUNT GAIL WAS GETTING READY
TO BAKE A BIRTHDAY CAKE.

I HAD AN IDEA!

WHY NOT MAKE SOUP?

LET'S SEE...I NEED A RECIPE.

JUST HOW DO WE MAKE
BIRTHDAY SOUP?

THINK BIRTHDAY! THINK SOUP!

HOW DO WE PUT THE TWO TOGETHER???

BUT,

FIRST

LET ME TELL YOU SOMETHING "BIG" ABOUT NOTHING:

DID YOU KNOW THAT JACK GOT OUT OF THE RECIPE BOX?

AND THE CAT THAT RAN AWAY WITH THE BIRTHDAY CAKE!

I COULD TELL YOU ABOUT
THE MOUSE THAT TOOK
THE CUP CAKE...

BUT, IT'S TIME TO MAKE
BIRTHDAY SOUP!

OH!
DID YOU HEAR ABOUT THE PINK ELEPHANT STANDING ON A BOX?

I COULD TELL YOU...

NO, IT'S A LONG STORY, AND IT'S TIME TO MAKE BIRTHDAY SOUP!

DO YOU KNOW ABOUT THE
BLUE RHINO THAT COULDN'T
FIND HIS MAMA?

SORRY,
I DON'T HAVE TIME TO TELL YOU
THAT STORY EITHER.

IT'S SOMEBODY'S BIRTHDAY SOMEWHERE AND I MUST MAKE BIRTHDAY SOUP!

THIS IS HOW YOU DO IT!

TO MAKE BIRTHDAY SOUP
YOU NEED A SCOOP

A SCOOP OF THIS AND A SCOOP OF THAT

IN A BOWL AS BIG AS A HAT

THEN,
YOU NEED SOMETHING ELSE
FROM THE SHELF

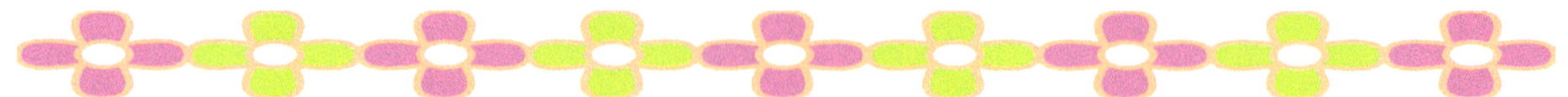

AND AFTER THAT,
YOU NEED
SOMETHING ELSE

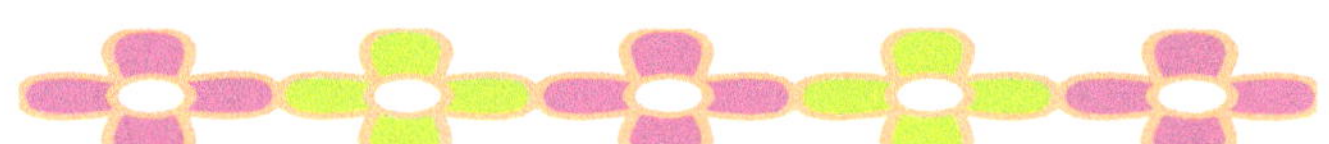

A LITTLE SALT
A LITTLE PEPPER

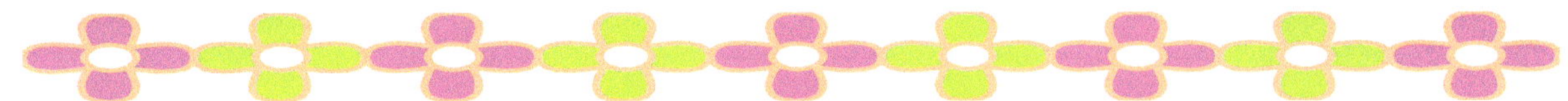

AND IT ALWAYS HELPS TO HAVE A HELPER

WHEN MAKING BIRTHDAY SOUP
FOR SOMEONE YOU LOVE

YOU CAN WEAR A HAT
BUT NOT A GLOVE

WEAR AN APRON
WITH LOTS OF BOWS

AND DON'T DROP ANYTHING
ON YOUR TOES

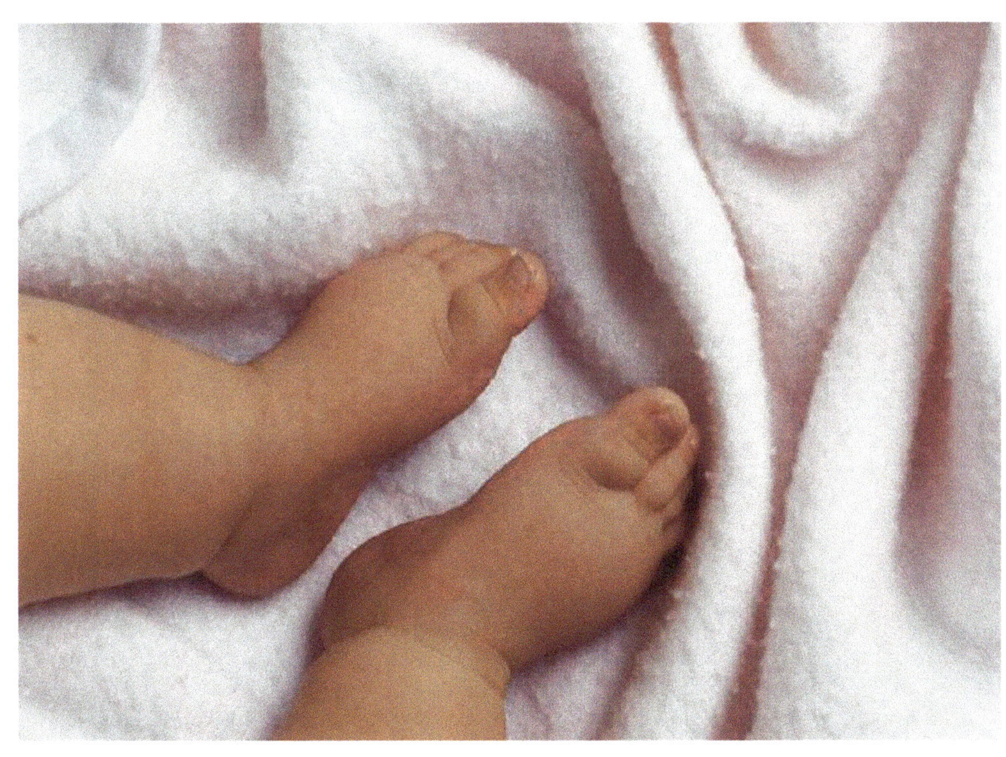

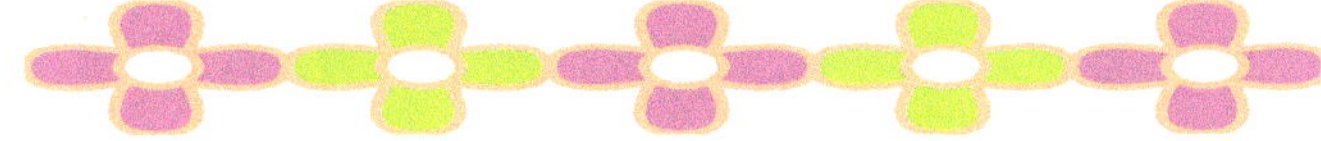

DON'T SPILL BIRTHDAY SOUP ON THE FLOOR

YOU WILL JUST HAVE TO MAKE SOME MORE

YOU CAN MAKE BIRTHDAY SOUP ANY DAY

HOORAY!!!

THAT YOU DON'T
GO OUTSIDE AND PLAY

BIRTHDAYS COME TO EVERYONE

SO
MAKING SOUP CAN BE FUN!!

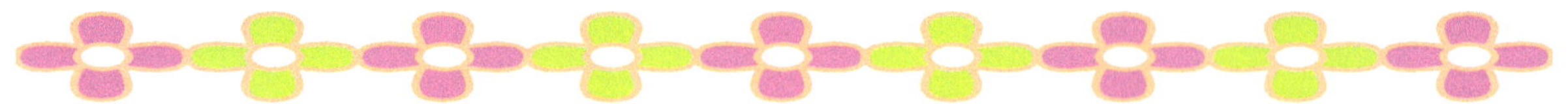

A big pot with good things in it
A big spoon to stir in it
A big smile to make it fun
A clock on the stove to shout

"It's done!"

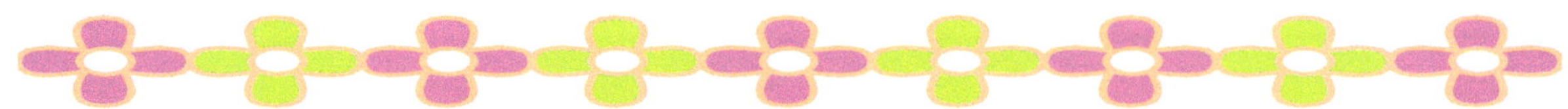

Aunt Gail's Post Script

A BIG pot with good things in it

A BIG spoon to stir in it

A big smile to make it fun

I love it when my sister helps me!

A clock on the stove

To shout

To shout

To shout

To shout

To shout

"It's done!"

TURN
THE
PAGE
FOR
MORE

Now, how do I keep my Daddy
and Big Brother from copying
my special Recipes?

I know, I will mail them to
Poppy and Grandmama

Or hide them in a secret place
where only Mama knows

If that doesn't work, I'll call
my uncle the professor

"This is how he really looks - on a good day!"

Here is a new birthday song that Uncle Hollis wrote.
He and Aunt Gail sang it for the very first time
at my sister, Jessica's, 8th birthday party, January 21, 2008.
My big brother, John Thomas,
and cousin, Connor, were there.
We had such fun!

A VERY SPECIAL DAY
(A new birthday song)
By Hollis L. Green

It's his/her birthday; it's his/her birthday,
It's a very special day;
It's his/her birthday; it's his/her birthday,
It's (name's) birthday today!

Some say it's just another day;
Others say it's a rainy day.
Some say it's a sunny day,
But it's a very special day;

It's his/her birthday; it's his/her birthday,
It is a very special day.
It's his/her birthday; it's his/her birthday,
It's (name's) birthday today!

The tune may be received by emailing a request to
GlobalEdAdvance@aol.com. Ask for the birthday song.

The Scoop About Birthday Soup
Dedicated to Erin Elizabeth Sise on her 9th birthday
September 25, 2007
Hollis L. Green

To make birthday soup
you need a scoop
A scoop of this and a scoop of that
In a BOWL as big as a hat

Then you need
something else from the shelf
And after that you need something else
A little salt a little pepper
And it always helps to have a helper

When making birthday soup
for someone you love
You can wear a hat but not a glove
Wear an apron with lots of bows
And don't drop anything on your toes
Don't spill birthday soup on the floor
You will just have to make some more

You can make birthday soup any day
That you don't go outside and play
Birthdays come to everyone
So making soup can be fun!

Order through Amazon.com, Barnes and Noble, Baker and Taylor,
or www.GlobalEdAdvance.org
Email: GlobalEdAdvance@aol.com
or any bookstore may order books through Ingram.

The Scoop About Birthday Soup
ISBN 978-0-9796019-8-9

GreenWine Family Books'
A division of
GlobalEdAdvancePress
37321-7635 USA